# Images of Irian

Photography by
Terry Owen

Text and Layout by
Terry Owen,
Richard Owen,
Gordon Greaves.

# Acknowledgements

This book has been a dream of mine for many years and its completion coincides with my departure from Irian Jaya after living here for twelve years. Completing this project over the past two years has involved many people and I would like to thank the following for their support.

Certainly without the support of P.T. Freeport Indonesia, I would not have been able to complete this book. I would especially like to thank Mr George Mealey for his support and encouragement over the past two years. I would also like to thank the heliops crew for their patience as we took detours while performing other assignments. Without the helicopter, seeing this country is a slow arduous task. Also Dave Francisco for his encouragement and support.

My first approach to a printer was an eye-opener and I wish to thank the members of Tien Wah Press that I worked with for their honest comments which sent us back to work for another six months. It was during this last revision that Gordon became part of the team. Gordon became an invaluable part of completing this book working with the final layout design and bringing life to many of the images with his captions. John Cutts also was key in providing opportunities to mix with the local Irianese population. My thanks to Dr. Tim Flannery for providing opportunities to get to know the fauna of Irian Jaya – a treasure by any standards. Early on, Richard picked up my outline and provided much of the text for the chapters. He also spent hours at scanning and layout work.

Without the support mentioned above, this book could not have happened. However, it would never have been anything but a dream if it were not for the belief in my photography and encouragement that publishing this book was a worthy goal.

So it is to my wife Linda that I dedicate this book, for without her I would not have taken up the challenge amid life's other responsibilities. Linda's love for nature has come to full bloom here in the tropical rainforest of Irian Jaya. Her love of God's little creatures is unmatched in anyone I have ever met. Through her I have been propelled into opportunities and visions for the land and fauna that I did not have before.

Linda's true testament to her love of the animals is evident in this book. The image of the Coppery Ringtail is the only known example of a hand-reared young successfully returned to the wild. That took six months of her life and several hours each day in the Montane rainforest researching his habits and obtaining his food supply.

May the completion of this work provide her the encouragement to grasp her vision and make it a reality.

© 1995 Ringtail Imagery

Printed in the Republic of Singapore

ISBN 0 646 22529 4

Ringtail Imagery
4025 East Chandler Blvd
#70-18A Phoenix Arizona
85044, USA

# Contents

# *Introduction*

Among the magnificent archipelago that lies southeast of Asia and north of Australia is an island whose uniqueness stands out like a brilliant gem. The second largest island in the world, and by far the largest of any of the tens of thousands that snake across the Pacific Ocean, New Guinea covers over 547,000 square kilometers of immensely diverse landscape. The western side of this island, which is governed by Indonesia, is called Irian Jaya, and contains one of the most diverse landscapes, and unique collections of flora on earth. A highly inhospitable climate and terrain intimidated most prospective colonization attempts, leaving it virtually untouched until midway into the 20th century. Until this time the population of indigenous people that sparsely inhabited this land had no outer influences, and they were left in a primitive, stone age culture, adding to the rarity of the area.

New Guinea, being geologically adolescent, is continually being remolded by the forces of nature. Fierce, overflowing rivers, due to intense amounts of rainfall, literally shift millions of tonnes of material annually, eroding and sculpturing the land. The convergence of three major tectonic plates just northeast of New Guinea add to the continual traumatization of this ever changing environment. Two glaciers, the Carstensz and Meren, remnants of a major glacier age, are other major implements to the changing of the many faceted features of Irian Jaya.

Irian Jaya's beauty lies in its varied aspects of land, people, and most particularly, plant and animal life. From the steamy mangrove swamps of the lowlands rise trees that seem to clutch at the sky, and their broad leaves create a canopy that is nearly impenetrable to the sun. The swamps give way to further rainforest that fades slowly at high altitudes to the cloud forests, whose interior is rarely without the shrouds of mist that spin about the vegetation, leaving thick moisture seeping from the dense mosses in the tops of the pygmy trees. As the air thins at altitudes above 2,750 meters, the thick forest vanishes leaving only grasslands. The grass gives way at over 4,250 meters, leaving the rock outcrops that harbor few plants. Those that do find root at such incredibly lifeless altitudes are rare, and beautiful when in bloom. These plants lie perhaps a few hundred yards from the ice of the retreating glaciers.

Mammals, though abundant, are scarcely seen in Irian Jaya, mostly restricted to marsupials, rodents, and bats. Large boars exist in the lowlands, and in the highlands there are smaller pigs as well as dingos. There is a large population of fabulous birds and reptiles. Insect species number in the hundred thousands, and there are some 800 species of arachnids. The most magnificent aspect of Irian Jaya, however, is the flora. The numbers of species of plants, many with medicinal values, are in the hundreds of thousands, and species are still being discovered and studied. Irian Jaya harbors one of the largest varieties of orchids in the world, as well as many more thousands of species of flora. The plants of Irian Jaya are a source of wonder, and are maintained in the island's very delicate habitat.

Nothing more is intended by this book than to present a brief glance at an overwhelmingly wondrous wilderness. It is a wilderness that has maintained through a changing world, leaving the veil of mystery that falls about it intact. This book is a glimpse of some of the splendor of the land. Unfortunately no amount of images in a book can properly capture the grandeur of this area. Hopefully, this book can spark the mind to project into these images the dimension that is missing.

## *Alpine*

The jagged peaks of Irian Jaya, in many places rising over 4,500 meters, form the backbone of the island. Seeming to clutch at the sky and pierce the dense cloud cover, they have in the past been a silent danger to pilots.

Glaciers remain in a very small area, and their strength over the centuries is obvious. The thick ice, carrying with it over its slow recession many tonnes of material, carved out the land leaving in its wake deeply cut valleys, and crystal lakes that mark the passage of immense power.

*One of the world's few remaining Equatorial Glaciers.*

*The icy surface of the Carstenz Glacier – the clarity evident here can be wiped away in a matter of minutes by fierce storms, with temperature changes in excess of 35º in 30 minutes.*

*Typical channel carved by the power of the glaciers in times past.*

*Marine fossil, located next to one of the glaciers at 4,420 meters.*

*An alpine meadow.*

The weather conditions can vary
tremendously over a distance of just
a few hundred meters.

*Alpine Lakes – remnants of the glaciers. On windless days the lakes act as mirrors for the rugged skyline beyond.*

*One of the highest lakes in Australasia nestles just below the edge of the Merrin Glacier and reflects the mighty peak of Puncak Jaya.*

*A silent, almost-forgotten memorial to the pioneers of aviation in this difficult area, the remains of a Douglas DC-3 still clutch the mountainside in a fatal embrace.*

*The locality of the DC-3 crash emphasizes the severity of the terrain in the area.*

*Alpine lakes, at altitudes up to 4,700 meters, host a surprising variety of animal and plant life in water that has very little movement and hovers near freezing year-round.*

*Natives use these valleys as a means of transiting the mountain range. The valley floors can vary from rock to swamp, with only the passage of time apparently making the difference. Few animals are found here, with various species of rats being predominant.*

*The major flora in some valleys is the* Cyathea *fern. Fed by the flow of water in crystal clear mountain streams, the ferns continue as a relic of the past.*

The rugged ridges of these mountains dominate the skyline and on a clear day the rocky peaks stretch to the horizon, seemingly challenging the endless stretch of sky. The peak of Mt. Zaagkam, as it is known by the local people whose view it dominates, rises 1,828 meters above the town of Tembagapura. Its face is exceedingly steep and rocky, and torrents of rain leave the face gushing with more than 60 waterfalls, some over 65 meters high. Behind this nearly vertical cliff face, Mt. Zaagkam is nothing more than an uplifted plate, with a fairly mild slope. These peaks seem to have been thrust from the ground with intense ferocity and they command the view about them.

*Mt. Zaagkam, late afternoon. Clouds fill the valley below, covering the town of Tembagapura.*

*The grandeur of the Carstenz Glacier forms a monumental backdrop for the Pandanus Palm.*

*Sunset outlines the mountain range, while the clouds*
*in the valley below form a sea of varying colors.*

Due to the afternoon cloud cover in the
highlands, sunsets are rare. When they occur,
however, they are often spectacular...

*The highest point in Australasia, Puncak Jaya, lies hidden behind the towering massif of the Jayawijaya Mountains. The peak
is one of the "Seven Summits", to which all serious sport mountaineers aspire – others include Everest and Kilimanjaro.*

*The cloud formations themselves can be beautiful,*
*ranging from wisps of white to dark thunderheads.*
*The varying foreground vegetation adds nature's*
*colorful counterpoint.*

*Seas of cloud below sunlit peaks create an eerie feeling.*

*Twin rainbows over Mt. Zaagkam produced by the setting sun – Christmas Eve, 1993.*

*A halo surrounds the rising moon as it makes a rare appearance through the jungle-clad mountainside.*

## *Montane Rainforest*

Below the rocky peaks of the Jayawijaya mountain range lie the lush alpine rainforests. Often called a moss or cloud forest, it is nearly always shrouded in mist, or dense clouds, and from the forest floor to the tops of the diminutive trees is coated with a thick layer of moss. The moss is continually saturated from the moisture of heavy mists or intense rainfall, and even on clear days, water falls from the tops of the trees like rain.

Nearly impossible to penetrate without the aid of carved trail or river, it is teeming with unknown flora of magnificent beauty. The forest is nothing more than a mass of green to the hurried and unconcentrated eye, but on closer inspection the strange ecosystem of the forest is an entirely new and mysterious world. Many unique plant forms exist, trees take on quite different shapes, and the life is without the usual uniformity of many forests. Plants live almost exclusively upon other plants (epiphitic life). The relationship between plants and animals is also amazing.

*The heavy moisture content in the air transforms a spider web into a natural representation of a crystal bowl.*

*Fungi, both edible and poisonous, abound in the rain forest where the rotting vegetation provides an ideal habitat.*

*Ever changing patterns are formed as the spiders and the rain combine in Nature's artwork.*

Rain falls from a
crystal blue sky,
a mist laden
breeze slides its
way through this
intricate labyrinth.

The voice of Aves
reverberates from
these moisture saturated
walls teeming with life.

Shadows of white
dissipate before the
horizontal rain,
and nature's rage thunders
about the forest of clouds.

Boundaries of reality
fade amongst this beauty.

Purifying chills slip
across humanity's spine
as nature caresses our
thoughts with these sights
of splendor from an
untouched world.

*Rich Owen*

*Trees like ghosts appear from the mist to greet the traveller in this land where only the birds can travel with ease.*

*Every shade of green is represented in the rainforest.*

*Amidst the greenery, flowers burst onto the scene to produce startling effects.*

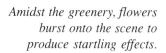

*Giant moths such as this Hercules are found in the rainforest, with wingspans of up to 20 centimeters.*

*Each droplet reflects the world around it, delicately poised and needing only a puff of wind or passer-by to shatter its beauty.*

The Ant Plant is a form of epiphitic life seen rarely – the plant uses a tree as its support, but takes no nutrients from it. Instead, a symbiotic relationship is formed with the ant population, which supplies the nutrients required in return for a dwelling place.

A Hercules moth rests on a leaf, patiently awaiting the night.

*Hidden away in the rainforest, until an errant ray of sunshine highlights the brilliant coloration.*

*Wood Swallows perch high in the branches of a dead tree like sentinels of the forest.*

*A Sacred Kingfisher rests momentarily on a slim branch. Rarely seen, these birds are nevertheless relatively common.*

*Against an azure sky, a bearded tree stands alone. The upper branches form a haven for a multitude of animal, bird, plant and insect life, living in harmony with each other and their surroundings. It is, however, a continuous fight for survival.*

*Orchids flourish in the rainforest
environment, with an enormous number of
known species, and probably as many more
as yet unknown to science. Most of the known
species are not found anywhere else.*

The orchids of the region present a
multitude of colors and shapes, some hardly
being recognizable as orchids at all.

A walk through the accessible parts of the rainforest will
bring the reward of startling bursts of color, some tucked
away in inconspicuous corners, others bursting from
tree trunks and branches.

*Rarely does sunlight penetrate the rainforest canopy; when it does, the colors change dramatically. It is more frequent to see misty backgrounds and a line of mountains marching off into the distance.*

Strangely shaped flowers can be found dotted
throughout the area, many alongside the roads.

*Patches of color mingle with the greens of the mosses*
*and the grey of the mist to produce a surreal image.*

*An unlikely pair of predators – the Common Tree Frog and the Pitcher Plant both prey on the bountiful insect population, the frog by direct attack and the plant by beguiling the insects with its attractive-smelling liquid lure.*

*The Silky Cuscus is a common highlands mammal, and often provides the natives with a tasty addition to their otherwise protein-poor diet. There are few natural predators, with wild dogs being the most dangerous threat. They are almost impossible to keep in captivity due to their continuously changing diet of various types of leaves.*

*The Coppery Ringtail Possum, like the Silky Cuscus, is common in the highlands and equally difficult to keep. Their inquisitive nature, poor eyesight and almost total lack of fear make them easy prey for natives and other predators alike. Extremely agile above ground, they are also surprisingly fast across the open areas between trees.*

*Until recently unknown to science, this tree kangaroo is regarded by the Moni tribe as sacred. It has two native names, the more common* Dingi So *meaning "Black One" and the alternate* Mbai So *which translates as "Forbidden One".*

*Lakes Paniai and Tigi are major natural features of the western portion of Irian Jaya. A center for the villagers from the surrounding areas is the town of Enarotali, on the eastern shore of Paniai, the seat of local government and home to over 5,000 people.*

Native villages dot the area. Hunting is a major occupation for the men, while the women work small garden areas perched on precipitous slopes. Traditional methods are used for hunting – the men are deadly accurate with their bows. Firearms are not used. The native costume suits the mid-altitude area, where temperatures vary only a few degrees year round and seasons are virtually unknown due to the proximity to the equator.

*A typical native settlement in the Baliem Valley.*

Highland rivers run through riverbeds that are both deep and wide, but the rivers, usually, are no larger than a stream. Over 510 centimeters of rain falls annually in the highlands area, and the streams fill the riverbeds, often overflowing and carrying many tonnes of material with them. Waterfalls are abundant in the steep highlands rivers, and in heavy rain they thunder with rage, water and earth crashes from heights sometimes exceeding 60 meters.

*Water cascades several hundred
meters down a sheer mountain wall
in the late afternoon sunlight.*

*Nearby is a colony of Mountain Swiftlets, a bird which lives in dark areas and uses sonar. A daytime insect-eater, the Swiflet is highly manoueverable and extremely fast. Bats share the same nesting area and hunt at night. Birds and bats co-exist peacefully.*

# *Lowlands*

The lowlands is predominantly a large flat expanse of land covered with thick jungle. From the coastline, tidal and mangrove swamps penetrate several miles inland. Due to the lack of slope on the land the lowland river systems are far more relaxed, lacking the raging turmoil of the highlands rivers. In heavy rainfall they carry thick sediment and soil out to the coast but do not have the power to move the many tonnes of rock that are carried by the highlands rivers.

Within this dense jungle is a spectacular ecosystem, but with it comes the sweltering heat and everpresent dangers of a tropical jungle system. Flowering plants of the lowlands are far more brilliant than those of the highlands. The myriad colours and flowers are spectacular, but most times are obscured by the mass of green. The number of species of birds in the lowland is far greater than that of the highlands – there are many birds that exist only on this island, and also many that are not native to the land, but now exist within the ecosystem.

There are several tribes that live in this area – one of the more prominent is the Asmat. They understand the land far better than perhaps anyone, and they know its dangers and mysteries. They commute the rivers and fish upon them in canoes fashioned from dugout logs. Balanced precariously upon the ends of their canoes they use poles to navigate the meandering, lazy rivers.

The transition from highlands to lowlands also brings a transition in both flora and fauna. Level ground allows the formation of plentiful lakes and associated plant growth, while the jungle itself becomes almost impenetrable due to heavy undergrowth and parasitic creepers.

*Native canoes are still manufactured by traditional methods – a single log, after painstaking work, provides both transportation and a fishing platform. The local people are renowned for the quality of their carving, which is also their major art form.*

*At Agats, the whole area is a tidal swamp. To move around their village the natives have built a complex system of walkways.*

*Twists and turns in the rivers are often hidden from the observer. It takes a skillful navigator to move from place to place using the waterways.*

*The serpentine twists and turns of the river system. As most transport is by boat, distances are often multiplied many times over. In most cases overland travel is impossible. Power canoes are beginning to appear in the area, with small outboard motors mounted on dugout canoes. Government and private enterprise also operate an increasing number of higher-technology watercraft, including air-cushion vehicles.*

*Large leaves provide protection for the local wildlife in the scorching rays of the sun. Other leaves are large enough to provide protection for the native population and are common in the lowland rainforest.*

*A quiet pool of water, tree stumps, orange fungus and bright leaves combine to produce a tranquil but unusual scene.*

*Trees grow above the surrounding canopy,
striving for the light that is denied them below.*

*Some of the more spectacular flowers in the lowlands
grow on trees rather than at ground level.*

*A rainforest tree is supported by its own buttresses, and in turn supports vines and other parasitic plants. Tree growth is often rapid, and the lowland timber is generally of a high quality. Indonesia does not permit clear-felling of timber, so the continuation of the rainforests is assured by law.*

*Butterflies and strange spiders display brilliant coloration as they rest, awaiting rays of sunshine or errant insects.*

*A spider (shown actual size) waits patiently for victims, which can include small birds. The arachnids are one of the most prevalent insect species in the mid- to low-altitude range.*

*Lowland orchids and brilliant flowers are as common as
their highland counterparts. Colors cover most of the
spectrum and provide a fascinating display.*

*As menacing as any crocodile or dinosaur, this rotting log and its reflection prowls a lowland pool...*

Birdlife is prevalent in the lowlands, with the egret being a familiar sight either fishing or perched on tree stumps observing the water. The hornbill is a common sight, usually appearing in small groups, while hawks and other raptors are also present in large numbers.

*Long sweeps of river, moving steadily to the sea, bring nourishment from the highlands to the lowlands rainforest and aquatic life.*

*Different species of butterfly gather together on a patch of ground that is secreting faint traces of desirable fragrances.*

*A tangled tracery of strangler vines surrounds a tree trunk, eventually killing the tree and leaving only a rotting framework on which the vine will continue to live for some time.*

*A dragonfly alights momentarily by the bank of a river.*

# *P.T. Freeport Indonesia*

New Guinea is an island rich in natural resources and populated, in many areas, by stone age cultures who had little contact with the modern world until after World War II. The natural resources have been a key element in providing help to these people.

For over 25 years, P.T. Freeport Indonesia has been active in Irian Jaya providing economic and social benefits to the Irianese people. Working with the government they have provided jobs and training programs allowing the Irianese to move into modern society. At the same time they have been strong advocates of maintaining the culture and arts of these local tribes. Support includes assistance in building schools and clinics in remote mountain villages.

Few places in the world put forth the challenges this company has met. It is possible, in the span of 115 kilometers, to journey from dense tropical swamps to sheer mountain peaks. Operating in this land means developing whatever roads or services are required, from housing and medical facilities to maintenance shops. From the air the road connecting these facilities looks like a thread woven in and out of a rough green fabric.

The mining operations are a result of exploration in 1936 by Jean-Jacques Dozy. However, it was not until the 1960's that technology provided the necessary support to meet the challenges of this land, culminating in the development of a world class mining operation.

*Viewed from 5,500 meters, the town of Tembagapura nestles between forbidding peaks. Home to over 9,000 people by December 1994, the town has grown from modest beginnings in the late 1960's to the thriving modern center that it is today. In this view can also be seen the Grasberg, Lake Wilson and the surrounding Mine offices, the Mill, Ridge Camp and the road disappearing into the Zaagkam Tunnel.*

*The first mine was the Ertsberg (Ore Mountain) – an outcrop of high grade copper ore. The Ertsberg Pit is now used to store water to operate the Mill in the valley below, and is known as Lake Wilson in honor of the Freeport pioneer, Forbes Wilson.*

*The main mining currently takes place at the Grasberg (Grass Mountain), one of the richest copper and gold reserves in the world, located at over 4,000 meters.*

*The Grasberg dwarfs the vehicle fleet working on it. The haul trucks are among the largest in the world, yet pale into insignificance compared to the sheer immensity of the Grasberg deposit and the surrounding peaks.*

*Working at the top of the world – the Grasberg open-pit mine is overshadowed by the remnants of the equatorial glaciers.*

*Like many other areas of the Freeport facility, the Big Gossan exploration camps were supported exclusively by helicopter.*

*The Mill currently processes in excess of 70,000 tonnes per day of ore (December 1994) with production to increase to over 115,000 tonnes per day in 1995.*

*The Mill is located at 2,590 meters. This is also the terminus of the road, with transport to the mine above being by cable car.*

*The Mill and Mine complex in 1980. At that time, daily throughput from the Mill averaged 8,100 tonnes per day, with the Grasberg yet to be investigated fully.*

*Ridge Camp, home to many of the Mine and Mill employees; also a major center for heavy equipment repair, welding and related industries.*

*Tembagapura in 1984, when production was just over 13,000 tonnes per day.*

*Tembagapura in 1994 with, to the left, the "suburb" of Hidden Valley.*

*Hidden Valley in the foreground, overlooking Tembagapura, with the road snaking its way beyond the town towards Ridge Camp, the Mill and the Mines.*

*Mile 50, where the gentle climb from the coast changes to a road so steep that only four-wheel-drive vehicles can traverse it.*

*The road approaches Mt. Zaagkam through typical alpine rainforest.*

*The safety barriers on the road protect vehicles from drops in excess of 1,000 meters.*

*The access road was a triumph of engineering when constructed in the late 1960's to early 1970's. In many places the road is carved out of the steep mountain side, while in others valleys had to be bridged to carry a single lane section of road.*

*Timika International Airport, with its 2,385 meter runway, is now capable of handling aircraft up to Boeing 757's – a far cry from the early days of the Fokker F-27. In the foreground, the Sheraton Inn Timika nestles in a jungle setting.*

*The workhorse of the operation – the helicopter. Their lifting ability and the skill of the pilots and engineers under extreme conditions made construction of the project possible.*

*Regular passenger transport to Australia and the rest of the Indonesian Archipelago is now carried out by a fleet of Boeing 737 aircraft.*

*The rugged terrain required new techniques in road building. Only a tiny fraction has been sealed, partly to stop it from sliding into the valley below! In the lowlands, many sections of road now "float" on a bed of recycled used tires, greatly improving the serviceability of the road and reducing maintenance.*

*The concentrated minerals are pumped down a 115 kilometer pipeline from the Mill to the deep-water port of Amamapare. Here the concentrate is dried in kilns and stored in barns awaiting shipment to smelters overseas.*

*The final part of the road was not completed until mid-1994. Until this time, road-building technology did not permit economical construction through the swamps, and transport between Amamapare and the rest of the project was by river.*

*Sunset over Amamapare.*

# Selected Reading Materials:

**Campbell, Julie**; *Irian Jaya*, Tyron Press, Scotland, 1991.

**Geoffrey S. Hope (Editor)**, Australian National University, **James A. Peterson,** Monash University, **Uwe Radok**, University of Melbourne, **Ian Allison**, Australian Government Dept. of Science; *The Equatorial Glaciers of New Guinea*, Results of 1971-1973 Australian Universities' expeditions to Irian Jaya: survey, glaciology, meteorology, biology and palaeoenvironments.

**Schneebaum, Tobias**; *Asmat Images*, Asmat Museum of Culture and Progress, 1985.

**Beehler, Bruce M.**; **Pratt, Thane K.**; **Zimmerman, Dale A.**; *Birds of New Guinea*, Princeton University Press, 1986.

**Turner, Keith**; **Smith, Steve**; *Birding in Irian Jaya*, S.W. Smith, 1992

**Rubeli, Ken**; *Tropical Rain Forest in South-East Asia – A Pictorial Journey*, Tropical Press SDN. BHD. Malaysia, 1986.

**Flannery, Timothy**; *Mammals of New Guinea*, Robert Brown & Associates Australia, 1990.

**Flannery, Timothy**; *The Future Eaters: An Ecological History of the Australasian Lands and People*, Reed, 1994.

**Beazley, Mitchell**; The World Conservation Union, *The Last Rainforests*, Mitchell Beazley Publishers, 1990.

**Pridgeon, Alec** (Editor); *What Orchid Is That?*, Weldon Publishing, Sydney, Australia, 1992.

**Miller, Andree**; *Orchids of Papua New Guinea (an introduction)*, Australian National University Press, Canberra, 1978.

**Mitton, Robert**; *The Lost World of Irian Jaya*, Oxford University Press, Melbourne, Australia, 1983.